BW
.99

W9-BCJ-777

WITHDRAWN

WITHDRAWN

Thoughts on Design

Paul Rand

Studio Vista
London

Van Nostrand Reinhold Company
New York

A Studio Vista Van Nostrand Reinhold
Art Paperback
Original edition Wittenborn Schultz, New York

Published in London 1970 by Studio Vista Limited
Blue Star House, Highgate Hill, London N19
and in New York by Van Nostrand Reinhold Company
450 West 33 Street, New York, NY 10001
Library of Congress Catalog Card Number 72-126307

Set in Linotype Bodoni Book
by Tri-Arts Press, New York, NY
Printed and bound in the Netherlands
by NV Drukkerij Reclame, Gouda

British SBN 289 79835 3 (paperback)
          289 79836 1 (hardbound)

Contents

Preface
to the third edition

In this edition of Thoughts on Design, the writer has made certain emendations. However, these do not materially alter his original thoughts or intentions. It is for the purpose of clarifying some of the ideas and enriching the visual material that a portion of the text has been revised and a number of illustrations have been replaced.

When this book was first written, it was the writer's intention to demonstrate the validity of those principles which, by and large, have guided artists (designers) since the time of Polycletus. The author believes that it is only in the application of those timeless principles that one can even begin to achieve a semblance of quality in one's work or understand the transient nature of the "fashionable." It is the continuing relevance of these principles that he wishes to emphasize, especially to those students and designers who have grown up in a world of pop and minimal art.

The author is indebted to all the advertisers, publishers, and manufacturers who have provided the opportunities for creating the visual material shown in this book. He also wishes to express his thanks to the typesetters and proofreaders for their help, and to the publishers for making a new edition of this book available.

P.R. Weston, Connecticut
January 1970

This book attempts to arrange in some logical order certain principles governing contemporary advertising design. The pictorial examples used to illustrate these principles are taken from work in which I was directly engaged. This choice was made deliberately and with no intention to imply that it represents the best translation of these principles into visual terms. There are artists and designers of great talent whose work would be perhaps more suitable. But I do not feel justified in speaking for them nor secure in attempting to explain their work without any possibility of misrepresentation. This is not to say that this book is purely the result of my efforts alone. I am indebted to many people — painters, architects, designers of past and present — for many theories and concepts. Many philosophers and writers, particularly John Dewey and Roger Fry, have helped to crystallize my thinking on the subject and to accelerate such progress as I have made. I have tried to pay my debt by quoting some of them.

P.R. New York City
January 1946

Graphic design—
which fulfills esthetic needs,
complies with the laws of form
and the exigencies of two-dimensional space;
which speaks in semiotics, sans-serifs,
and geometrics;
which abstracts, transforms, translates,
rotates, dilates, repeats, mirrors,
groups, and regroups—
is not good design
if it is irrelevant.

Graphic design—
which evokes the symmetria of Vitruvius,
the dynamic symmetry of Hambidge,
the asymmetry of Mondrian;
which is a good gestalt;
which is generated by intuition or by computer,
by invention or by a system of co-ordinates—
is not good design
if it does not co-operate
as an instrument
in the service of communication.

Visual communications of any kind, whether persuasive or informative, from billboards to birth announcements, should be seen as the embodiment of form and function: the integration of the beautiful and the useful. In an advertisement, copy, art, and typography are seen as a living entity; each element integrally related, in harmony with the whole, and essential to the execution of the idea. Like a juggler, the designer demonstrates his skills by manipulating these ingredients in a given space. Whether this space takes the form of advertisements, periodicals, books, printed forms, packages, industrial products, signs, or TV billboards, the criteria are the same.

That the separation of form and function, of concept and execution, is not likely to produce objects of esthetic value has been repeatedly demonstrated. Similarly, it has been shown that the system which regards esthetics as irrelevant, which separates the artist from his product, which fragments the work of the individual, which creates by committee, and which makes mincemeat of the creative process will, in the long run, diminish not only the product but the maker as well.

John Dewey, commenting on the relationship between fine art and useful or technological art, says: "That many, perhaps most, of the articles and utensils made at present for use are not genuinely esthetic happens, unfortunately, to be true. But it is true for reasons that are foreign to the relation of the 'beautiful' and 'useful' as such. Wherever conditions are such as to prevent the act of production from being an experience in which the whole creature is alive and in which he possesses his living through enjoyment, the product will lack something of being esthetic. No matter how useful it is for special and limited ends, it will not be useful in the ultimate degree—that of contributing directly and liberally to an expanding and enriched life."[1]

1. John Dewey
   Art as Experience, p. 26
   Etherial Things

The esthetic requirements to which Dewey refers are, it seems to me, exemplified in the work of the Shakers. Their religious beliefs provided the fertile soil in which beauty and utility could flourish. Their spiritual needs found expression in the design of fabrics, furniture, and utensils of great esthetic value. These products are a document of the simple life of the people, their asceticism, their restraint, their devotion to fine craftsmanship, and their feeling for proportion, space, and order.

Ideally, beauty and utility are mutually generative. In the past, rarely was beauty an end in itself. The magnificent stained glass windows of Chartres were no less utilitarian than was the Parthenon or the Pyramid of Cheops. The function of the exterior decoration of the great Gothic cathedrals was to invite entry; the rose windows inside provided the spiritual mood. Interpreted in the light of our own experiences, this philosophy still prevails.

Parthenon, Athens
447-432 B.C.

The Designer's
Problem

An erroneous conception of the graphic designer's function is to imagine that in order to produce a "good layout[1]" all he need do is make a pleasing arrangement of miscellaneous elements. What is implied is that this may be accomplished simply by pushing these elements around, until something happens. At best, this procedure involves the time-consuming uncertainties of trial and error, and at worst, an indifference to plan, order or discipline.

11

1. Because of its popular acceptance, the term layout is used. Unfortunately, a layout is deprecatingly interpreted as a blueprint for an illustration. I should prefer to use composition in the same sense in which it is used in painting

The designer does not, as a rule, begin with some preconceived idea. Rather, the idea is (or should be) the result of careful study and observation, and the design a product of that idea. In order, therefore, to achieve an effective solution to his problem, the designer must necessarily go through some sort of mental process.[2] Consciously or not, he analyzes, interprets, formulates. He is aware of the scientific and technological developments in his own and kindred fields. He improvises, invents or discovers new techniques and combinations. He co-ordinates and integrates his material so that he may restate his problem in terms of ideas, signs, symbols, pictures. He unifies, simplifies, and eliminates superfluities. He symbolizes — abstracts from his material by association and analogy. He intensifies and reinforces his symbol with appropriate accessories to achieve clarity and interest. He draws upon instinct and intuition. He considers the spectator, his feelings and predilections.

2. The reader may wish to refer to R.H.Wilenski. The Modern Movement in Art for a description of the artist's mental processes in creating a work of art

The designer is primarily confronted with three classes of material: a) the given material: product, copy, slogan, logotype, format, media, production process; b) the formal material: space, contrast, proportion, harmony, rhythm, repetition, line, mass, shape, color, weight, volume, value, texture; c) the psychological material: visual perception and optical illusion problems, the spectators' instincts, intuitions, and emotions as well as the designer's own needs.

As the material furnished him is often inadequate, vague, uninteresting, or otherwise unsuitable for visual interpretation, the designer's task is to re-create or restate the problem. This may involve discarding or revising much of the given material. By analysis (breaking down of the complex material into its simplest components...the how, why, when, and where) the designer is able to begin to state the problem.

Because advertising art, in the end, deals with the spectator, and
because it is the function of advertising to influence him, it follows
that the designer's problem is twofold: to anticipate the spectator's re-
actions and to meet his own esthetic needs. He must therefore dis-
cover a means of communication between himself and the spectator
(a condition with which the easel painter need not concern himself). The problem is not simple; its very complexity virtually dictates
the solution — that is, the discovery of an image universally com-
prehensible, one which translates abstract ideas into visual forms.

It is in symbolic, visual terms that the designer ultimately realizes his
perceptions and experiences; and it is in a world of symbols that
man lives. The symbol is thus the common language between artist and
spectator. Webster defines the symbol as "that which stands for or
suggests something else by reason of relationship, association, con-
vention, or accidental but not intentional resemblance; especially,
a visible sign of something invisible, as an idea, a quality or totality
such as a state or a church; an emblem; as, the lion is the *symbol*
of courage; the cross is the *symbol* of Christianity. 'A *symbol* is a
representation which does not aim at being a reproduction.' (Goblet
d'Alvielle)."

Words like simplified, stylized, geometric, abstract, two-dimensional,
flat, non-representational, non-mimetic are commonly associated,
sometimes incorrectly, with the term symbol. It is true that the depic-
tion of most distinctive symbols does fit the image these words
help to characterize visually; but it is not true that the symbol has to
be simplified (etc.) in order to qualify as a symbol. The fact that
some of the best symbols are simplified images merely points to the
effectiveness of simplicity but not to the meaning of the word
per se. In essence, it is not what it looks like but what it does that
defines a symbol. A symbol may be depicted as an "abstract" shape,
a geometric figure, a photograph, an illustration, a letter of the
alphabet, or a numeral. Thus, a five-pointed star, the picture of a
little dog listening to his master's voice, a steel engraving of
George Washington, or the Eiffel Tower itself—are all symbols!

13

Religious and secular institutions have clearly demonstrated the power of the symbol as a means of communication. It is significant that the crucifix, aside from its religious implications, is a demonstration of perfect form as well — a union of the aggressive vertical (male) and the passive horizontal (female). It is not too farfetched to infer that these formal relations have at least something to do with its enduring quality. Note the curious analogy between Occidental and Oriental thought from the following excerpts: Rudolf Koch, in *The Book of Signs*, comments: "In the origin of the Cross, God and earth are combined and are in harmony . . . from two simple lines a complete sign has been evolved. The Cross is by far the earliest of all signs and is found everywhere, quite apart from the concepts of Christianity." In the *Book of Changes* (Chou Yih) it is stated: "The fathomlessness of the male and female principles (Yang and Yin) is called God." This conception is illustrated by the Taichi symbol expressing the "two regulating powers which together create all the phenomena of Nature." The essence of Chinese philosophy is revealed in the expression: "All things are produced by the action of the male and female principles."

. . . In this illustration the form is intensified by dramatic narrative association. The literal meaning changes according to context; the formal quality remains unchanged.

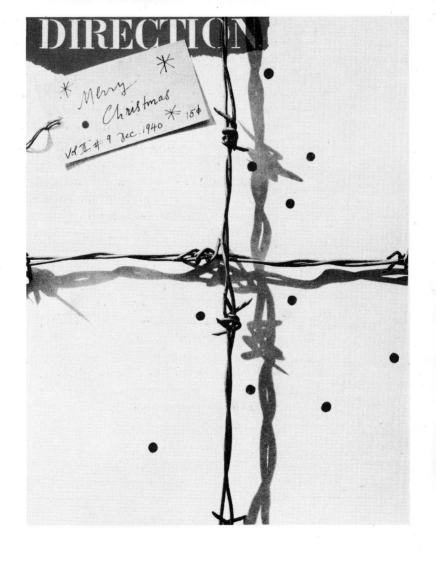

Magazine cover
red and black on white
1940

15

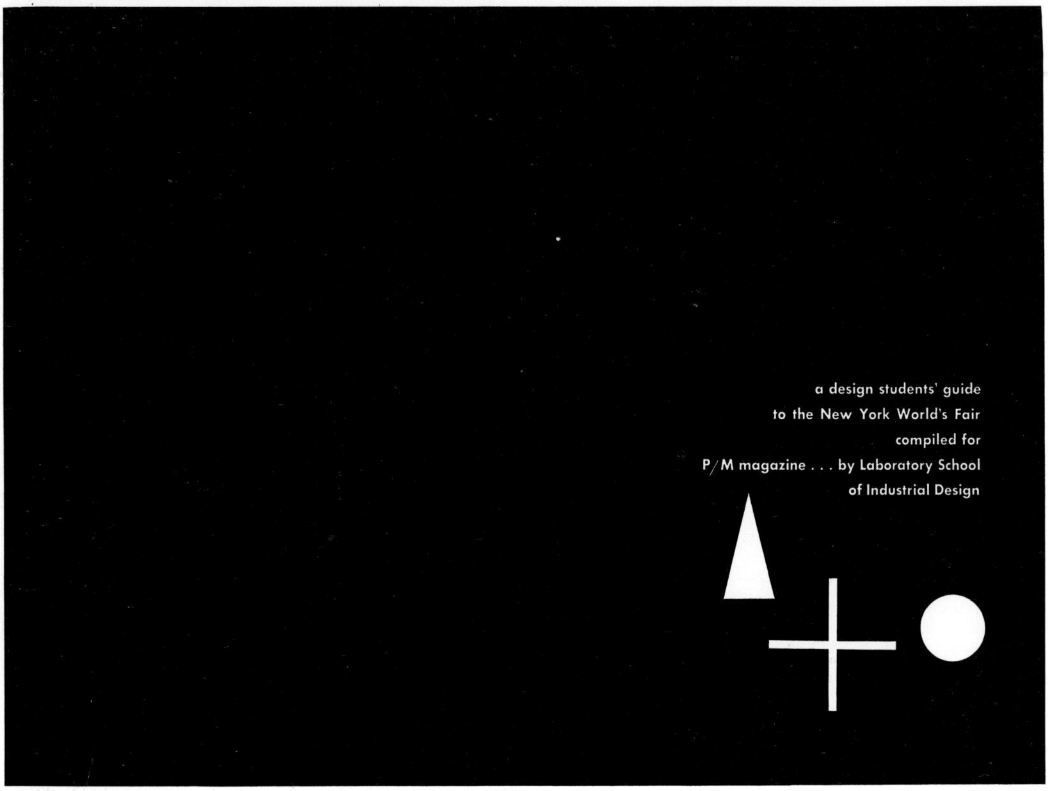

a design students' guide
to the New York World's Fair
compiled for
P/M magazine . . . by Laboratory School
of Industrial Design

Booklet cover
black and white
1939

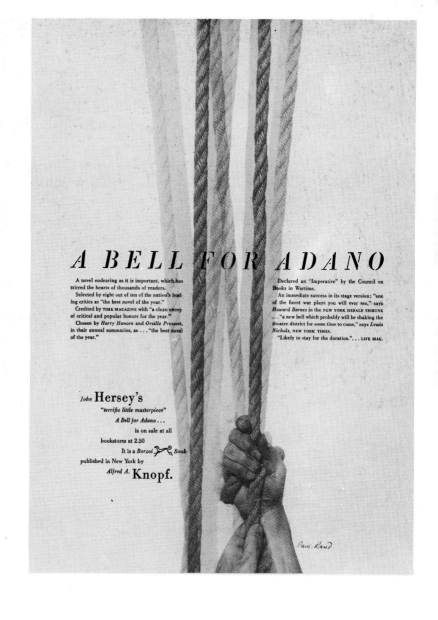

Magazine advertisement
Alfred A. Knopf
February 1945

**Versatility
of the Symbol**

The same symbol is potentially a highly versatile device, which can be used to illustrate many different ideas. By juxtaposition, association, and analogy, the designer is able to manipulate it, alter its meaning, and exploit its visual possibilities.

Distinguishing between the literal and plastic meaning of images, Ozenfant declares: "Every form has its specific mode of expression (the language of plastic) independent of its purely ideological significance (language of the sign)."[1] The circle as opposed to the square, for instance, as a pure form evokes a specific esthetic sensation; ideologically it is the symbol for eternity, without beginning or end. A red circle may be interpreted as the symbol of the sun, the Japanese battle flag, a stop sign, an ice-skating rink, or a special brand of coffee... *depending on its context.*

1. Amedee Ozenfant
   Foundations of Modern Art
   p. 249

Perfume bottle,
gold wire and crystal
1944

Trademark
Colorforms
1959

Trademark
Consolidated Cigar Co.
1959

Trademark
American Broadcasting Co.
1962

19

Brochure
black and yellow, Autocar
1942

Illustration
GHP Cigar Company
1952

21

The Role of Humor

Readership surveys demonstrate the magnetic force of humor in the field of visual communication, in advertising, editing, and in a multitude of miscellaneous design problems. The reference is not principally to cartoon strip advertisements, nor to out-and-out gags, but to a more subtle variety, one indigenous to the design itself and achieved by means of juxtaposition, association, size, relationship, proportion, space or special handling.

The visual message which professes to be profound or elegant often boomerangs as mere pretension; and the frame of mind which looks at humor as trivial and flighty mistakes the shadow for the substance. In short, the notion that the humorous approach to visual communication is undignified or belittling is sheer nonsense. This misconception has been discredited by those advertisers and publishers who have successfully exploited humor as a means of creating an atmosphere of confidence, good will, good fellowship, and the *right frame of mind* toward an idea or product. Radio and TV commercials have made tremendous strides in the use of humor as a potent sales device. And, as an aid to understanding serious problems in war training, as an effective weapon in safety posters,[1] war bond selling, and morale building, humor was neglected neither by government nor civilian agencies during the second World War.

Stressing the profound effects of entertainment, Plato, in *The Republic*, declares: "Therefore do not use compulsion, but let early education be rather a sort of amusement..." The arts of ancient China,[2] India, and Persia reflect a humorous spirit in the design of masks, ceramics, and paintings. American advertising in its infancy also demonstrated this tendency toward humor: the cigar store Indian, the medicine man. And that humor is a product of serious contemporary thought is revealed in the significant paintings and sculpture of our time. "True humor," says Thomas Carlyle, "springs not more from the head than from the heart; it is not contempt, its essence is love, it issues not in laughter, but in still smiles, which lie far deeper."

1. Printers' Ink
December 28, 1945

2. Roger Fry, Transformations
Some Aspects
of Chinese Art, pp. 79-81

Cover design, red and green
American Institute of Graphic Arts
1968

Paul Rand

One sheet poster
full color, Interfaith Movement
1954

Magazine cover
pink, tan, and black
1954

Illustration
Smith Kline & French
1945

Exhibition poster
IBM Gallery, full color
1970

26

Corona 3 for 50¢

Newspaper advertisement
El Producto Cigar Co.
1957

The kind of humor expressed by the "Dubonnet man" (originated by Cassandre) is inherent in the design itself. The "funny" face and general attitude seem to *suggest* rather than *illustrate* a quality of conviviality. To adapt this figure for an American audience, the problem was to impart this same spirit without altering the original visual conception.

Magazine advertisement
detail, Dubonnet Corporation
1942

Magazine advertisement
montage, full color
1943

SPRING

Paul Rand

Exposicion
de pintura
contemporanea
norteamericana.

...The "visual pun," in which a double meaning is projected graphically, can be as informative as it is entertaining.

Poster
color montage, Apparel Arts
1939

Poster, color montage
Museum of Modern Art
project, 1941

31

orpi[*]

permanent oil colors
made in the U.S.A.
by the manufacturers
of the
Rembrandt colors
studio tubes
.25 .35 .50
3 inch tubes .10 .15
Talens & Son, Inc.
Newark, N. J.
write for color card

*original Holland formulae

Magazine advertisement
black and white, Talens & Sons
1942

Cover design
red and black
1949

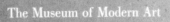
The Museum of Modern Art

Modern Art in Your Life

From the Menarche to the Menopause . . . Woman requires 4 times as much iron as man.

Folder, red, green, black
Smith Kline & French
1946

Cover
black and white, Direction
1941

Magazine cover
red and green
1939

Imagination and the Image

Frequently, trite ideas or unimaginative translation of those ideas is the result not of poor subject matter but of poor interpretation of a problem. In the absence of a fresh, visual solution, subject matter sometimes becomes the scapegoat. Such difficulties may arise if: a) the designer has interpreted a commonplace idea with a commonplace image; b) he has failed to resolve the problem of integrating form and content; or c) he has failed to interpret the problem as a two-dimensional organization in a given space. He has thus deprived his visual image of the potential to suggest, perhaps, more than the eye can see. And he has denied himself the opportunity of saying the commonplace in an uncommonplace way.

Roger Fry, commenting on the problem of integrating representational and plastic elements, states: "This may, perhaps, give us a hint as to the nature of such combinations of two arts, namely, that co-operation is most possible where neither of them are pushed to the fullest possibilities of expression, where in both a certain freedom is left to the imagination, where we are moved rather by suggestion than statement."[1]

1. Roger Fry
Transformations
Some Questions in Esthetics
p. 24

Visual statements such as illustrations which do not involve esthetic judgment and which are merely literal descriptions of reality can be neither intellectually stimulating nor visually distinctive. By the same token, the indiscriminate use of type faces, geometric patterns, and "abstract" shapes (hand or computer generated) is self-defeating when they function merely as a vehicle for self-expression. The visual statement, on the other hand, which seeks to express the essence of an idea, and which is based on function, fantasy, and analytic judgment, is likely to be not only unique but meaningful and memorable as well.

In practice, when an advertisement is submitted for approval, it is prettied up with mat and cellophane and judged as an isolated fragment. Under such conditions, and in the absence of competition, the purely conventional type of illustration may seem quite effective. However, for an advertisement to hold its own in a competitive race, the designer must steer clear of visual clichés by some unexpected interpretation of the commonplace. He does this partly by simplifying, by abstracting, by symbolizing. If the resulting visual image is in any way ambiguous, it may be supplemented by one which is more clearly recognizable. In the examples which follow, the abstract, geometric forms (attention-arresting devices) tend to dominate, while the photographic images play a supporting role.

24 sheet poster
20th Century Fox
1950

Cover design
blue, terra cotta, black
1958

...There are, however, instances when recognizable images are of sufficient plastic expressiveness to make the addition of geometric or 'abstract' shapes superfluous.

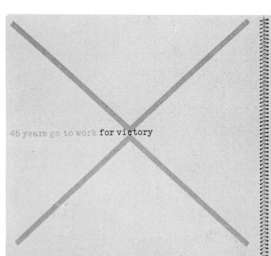

45 years go to work for victory

From its very inception in 1897 every Autocar activity has trained the Company for its vital role in the war program. For 45 years without interruption it has manufactured motor vehicles exclusively, concentrating in the last decade on heavy-duty trucks of 5 tons or over. For 45 years Autocar has pioneered the way, developing many history-making "firsts" in the industry: the first porcelain spark-plug; the first American shaft-driven automobile; the first double reduction gear drive; the first circulating oil system. For 45 years Autocar insistence on mechanical perfection has wrought a tradition of precision that is honored by every one of its master workers. These are achievements that only time can win. The harvest of these years, of this vast experience, is at the service of our government. Autocar is meeting its tremendous responsibility to national defense by putting its 45 years' experience to work in helping to build for America a motorized armada such as the world has never seen.

Brochure
black and yellow, Autocar
1942

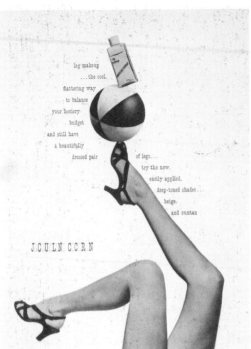

Advertisement
tan and black, Jacqueline Cochran
1944

Magazine cover
full color, Curtis Publishing Company
1956

Newspaper advertisement
black and white, Orbach's
1946

if only you
could be seen
in lingerie*
from Ohrbach's!

Ohrbach's
14th Street facing Union Square
Newark store: Market and Halsey Streets
"A business in millions... a profit in pennies"

Magazine cover
pink and olive green
1943

To Catch a Hummingbird

Westinghouse

Suppose you had to capture alive one little hummingbird
flying a known course high over the Amazon jungle.
Difficult? Sure, but no more so than the job assigned to a new
radar system Westinghouse is building for the
NASA-Gemini space program.
The bird is an Agena rocket, orbiting the earth at 17,500 miles
per hour. The hunter, in an intersecting orbit, is the
Gemini two-man spacecraft being built by McDonnell Aircraft.
And so the hunt begins. The spacecraft radar finds
the target and starts an electronic question-and-answer game.
A computer keeps score, giving the astronauts continuous
readings on angles and approach speeds until the vehicles are
joined. The hummingbird is caught.
The Gemini experiments will be a prelude to the first
moon trip. And Westinghouse is already working on advanced
radar systems for lunar landings and deep space missions.
You can be sure . . . if it's Westinghouse.

Magazine advertisement
full color, Westinghouse
1963

43

Magazine cover
black and green, Apparel Arts
1939

Book jacket
Wittenborn & Schultz
1946

It is a truism that the fundamental problem of the advertiser and publisher is to get the message into the reader's mind. Commonplace images and unimaginative visualization afford the spectator little reason for becoming engrossed in an advertiser's product. Radio and TV advertisers, who use media by which it is possible for studio and home spectators to take part in the proceedings, have discovered the value of audience participation. Producers of print advertising, on the other hand, must devise methods of engaging the eye and attention of the reader in a manner consistent with the printed form. Picture puzzles, cryptograms, quizzes, memory tests, and teaser devices have been employed to this end from time to time.

Contemporary advertising techniques, resulting from experiments and discoveries in the fields of psychology, art, and science, suggest many possibilities. Among the great contributions to visual thought is the invention of collage. Collage and montage permit the showing of seemingly unrelated objects or ideas as a single picture; they enable the designer to indicate simultaneous events or scenes which by more conventional methods would result in a series of isolated pictures. Compactness of the complex message in a single picture more readily enables the spectator to focus his attention on the advertiser's message.

Contemporary as it may seem, the concept of simultaneity takes us back to ancient China. The Chinese, aware of the need for a means of expressing in one picture simultaneous actions or multiple events, devised a form of oblique projection. They also devised a means of showing one object behind, above, or below another, by free disposition of elements in a composition, completely disregarding the illusions of visual perspective. This was essentially a method of formalizing or "neutralizing" the object. It was a transformation resulting in formal arrangements rather than conventional illustration. In one sense montage and collage are integrated visual arrangements in space, and in another sense, absorbing visual tests which the

Magazine advertisement
full color
1946

spectator may perceive and decipher for himself. He may thus participate directly in the creative process.

Poster
full color, Apparel Arts
1940

Magazine advertisement
full color, Olivetti
1953

THOMAS ERSKINE on the Advantages of Free Speech

When men can freely communicate their thoughts and their sufferings, real or imaginary, their passions spend themselves in air, like gunpowder scattered upon the surface; but pent up by terrors, they work unseen, burst forth in a moment, and destroy everything in their course.

(Rex v.Paine,1792)

Magazine advertisement
full color, Container Corporation
1954

Magazine advertisement
full color, montage
1964

Magazine cover
red and black
1939

54

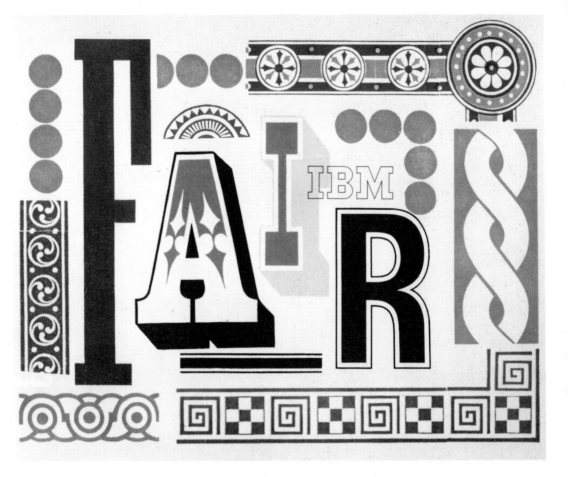

Cover design
full color, IBM
1964

55

The idea of the photogram or cameraless photography goes back as far as the 18th century. In our time the pioneers of photography without the use of a camera were Man Ray in France, Lissitzky in Russia, and Moholy-Nagy in Germany. One of the first to apply this technique in advertising art was the constructivist, El Lissitzky, who, in 1924, designed a poster for Pelikan inks. Picasso, at a later date, also made use of the photogram. In advertising, the photogram has yet to be fully exploited.

Although the effectiveness of the photogram depends chiefly on straightforward mechanical methods (light on sensitized paper), it offers the designer ample opportunity for esthetic, manual control. In a sense, it is not a picture of the object, but the object itself; and, as in stroboscopic photography, it makes picturization of continuous movement possible. Although some of its effects may be approximated with pen, brush, or scissors, the quality inherent in the subtle light modulations can be achieved only by means of the photogram. The following illustrations will help to point out the qualitative differences between the photogram and other techniques.

Package design
photogram and color
1952

Photogram
book jacket
1943

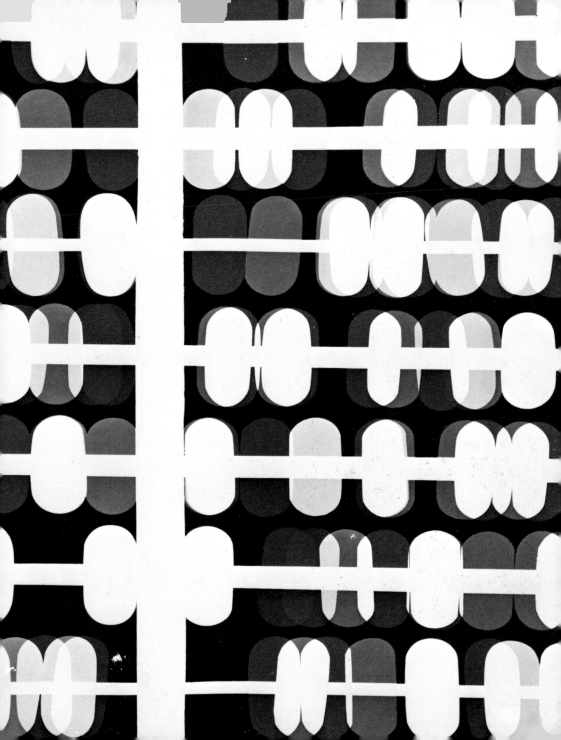

Book jacket
blue and black, Wittenborn & Schultz
1951

58

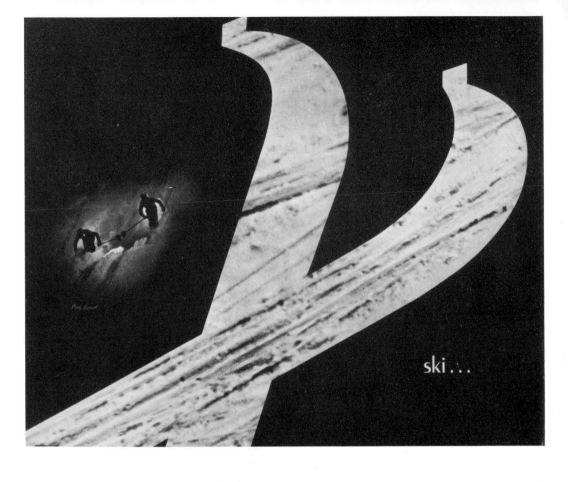

ski . . .

Title page
photomontage, Esquire
1938

59

going back to school...

Title page
black and yellow, Esquire
1939

Book jacket
black, red, green, and brown
1946

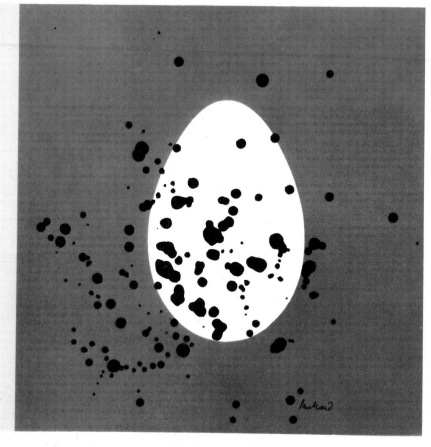

Sources and Resources
of 20th Century Design

June 19 to 24, 1966
The International Design
Conference in Aspen

Poster
red and black
1966

62

The emotional force generated by the repetition of words or pictures and the visual possibilities (as a means of creating texture, movement, rhythm, indicating equivalences for time and space) should not be minimized.

The following are but a few instances of our everyday experiences in which the magical, almost hypnotic, effects of repetition operate: the exciting spectacle of marching soldiers, in the same dress, same step, and same attitude; the fascination of neatly arranged flower beds of like color, structure, and texture; the impressive sight of crowds at football games, theatres, public demonstrations; the satisfaction we derive from the geometric patterns created by ballet dancers and chorus girls with identical costumes and movements; the feeling of order evoked by rows of methodically placed packages on the grocer's shelf; the comforting effect of the regularity of repeat patterns in textiles and wallpapers; the excitement we experience at the sight of plane formations or birds in flight.

Package design
cerise and black, IBM
1956

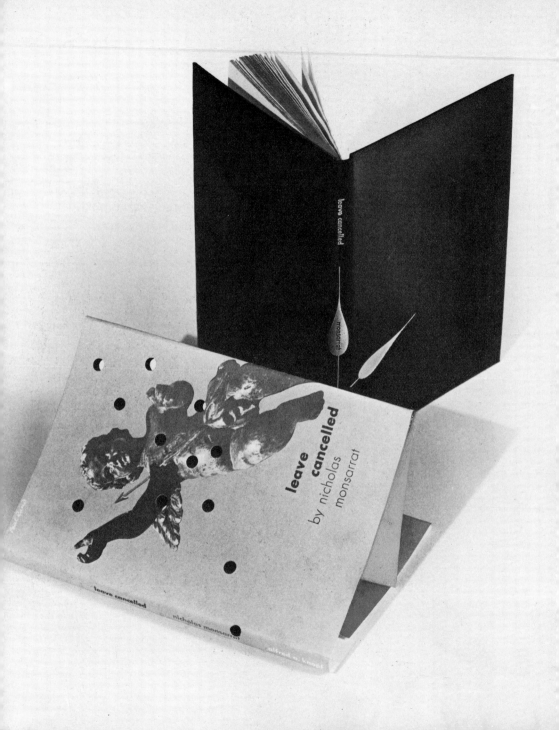

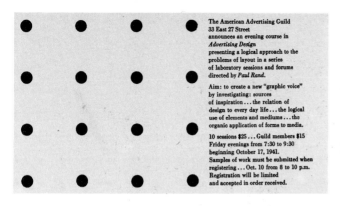

The American Advertising Guild
33 East 27 Street
announces an evening course in
Advertising Design
presenting a logical approach to the
problems of layout in a series
of laboratory sessions and forums
directed by *Paul Rand*.

Aim: to create a new "graphic voice"
by investigating: sources
of inspiration ... the relation of
design to every day life ... the logical
use of elements and mediums ... the
organic application of forms to media.

10 sessions $25 ... Guild members $15
Friday evenings from 7:30 to 9:30
beginning October 17, 1941.
Samples of work must be submitted when
registering ... Oct. 10 from 8 to 10 p.m.
Registration will be limited
and accepted in order received.

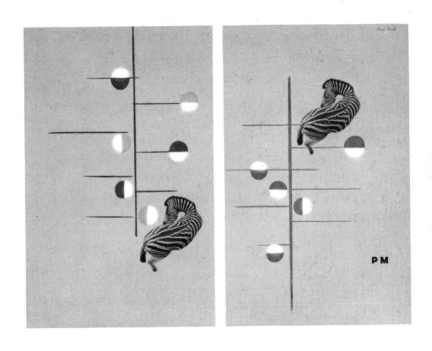

Jacket and binding
pink, green, and gold
1945

Announcement
black and white
1941

Magazine cover
full color, PM
1938

Brochure cover
full color, U.S. Navy
1959

Our custom is limited to those few
men in each community who want a
finer hat...and to whom price is secondary

Disney, *Hatmaker since* 1885

Magazine advertisement
black and tan, Disney
1946

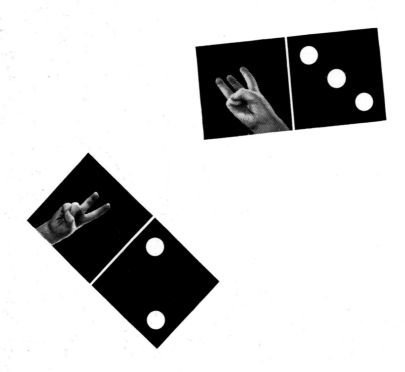

Illustration
SKF Laboratories
1946

Wall covering
gray and black, IBM
1957

68

Advertisement
illustration, Westinghouse
1968

70

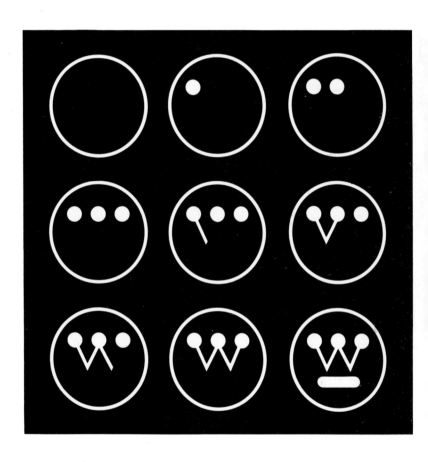

Trademark
TV billboard, Westinghouse
1961

71

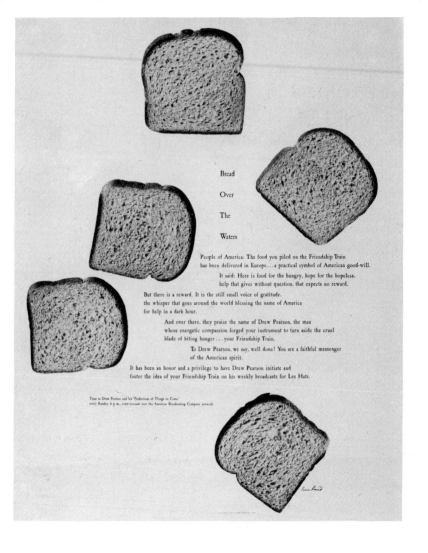

Bread

Over

The

Waters

People of America: The food you piled on the Friendship Train
has been delivered in Europe...a practical symbol of American good-will.

It said: Here is food for the hungry, hope for the hopeless,
help that gives without question, that expects no reward.

But there is a reward. It is the still small voice of gratitude,
the whisper that goes around the world blessing the name of America
for help in a dark hour.

And over there, they praise the name of Drew Pearson, the man
whose energetic compassion forged your instrument to turn aside the cruel
blade of biting hunger ... your Friendship Train.

To Drew Pearson, we say, well done! You are a faithful messenger
of the American spirit.

It has been an honor and a privilege to have Drew Pearson initiate and
foster the idea of your Friendship Train on his weekly broadcasts for Lee Hats.

Tune in Drew Pearson and his "Predictions of Things to Come"
every Sunday, 6 p.m., coast-to-coast over the American Broadcasting Company network.

Newspaper advertisement
Frank H. Lee Co.
1947

Newspaper advertisement
black and white
1954

72

To the executives and management of the Radio Corporation of America:

Messrs. Alexander, Anderson, Baker, Buck, Cahill, Cannon, Carter, Coe, Coffin, Dunlap, Elliott, Engstrom, Folsom, Gorin, Jolliffe, Kayes,

Marek, Mills, Odorizzi, Orth, Sacks, Brig. Gen. Sarnoff, R. Sarnoff, Saxon, Seidel, Teegarden, Tuft, Watts, Weaver, Werner, Williams

Gentlemen: An important message intended expressly for your eyes is now on its way to each one of you by special messenger.

William H. Weintraub & Company, Inc.   *Advertising*   *488 Madison Avenue, New York*

Disputes arising between the two schools of typographic thought, the *traditional* on the one hand and the *modern* on the other, are, it seems to me, the fruits of misplaced emphasis. I believe the real difference lies in the way 'space' is interpreted: that is, the way in which an image is placed on a sheet of paper. Such incidental questions as the use of sans-serif type faces, lower case letters, ragged settings, primary colors, etc., are at best variables, which merely tend to sidetrack the real issue.

'But great original artists,' says John Dewey, 'take a tradition into themselves. They have not shunned but digested it. Then the very conflict set up between it and what is new in themselves and in their environment creates the tension that demands a new mode of expression.' Understanding modern and traditional in this light, the designer is able to bring into a new and logical relationship traditional graphic forms and ideas together with 'new' concepts based on a present-day point of view. This union of two supposedly divergent forces provides conditions which lead to fresh visual experiences.

In advertising one is often faced with the problem of conveying a quality of age. In the example which follows, traditional 'ornaments' combine with geometric forms to establish new relationships. This transition from old to new may be accomplished by arranging these familiar devices in some surprising manner:

Book cover
red and yellow, Wittenborn & Schultz
1944

Label designs
full color, Schenley
1942

74

Typographic Form
and Expression

One of the objectives of the designer who deals with type matter
concerns readability. Unfortunately, however, this function is often
overemphasized at the expense of style, individuality, and the very
effectiveness of the printed piece itself.

By carefully arranging type areas, spacing, size, and 'color,' the
typographer is able to impart to the printed page a quality which helps
to dramatize the contents. He is able to translate type matter into
tactile patterns. By concentrating the type area and emphasizing the
margin (white space), he can reinforce, by contrast, the textural
quality of the type. The resulting effect on the reader may be properly
compared to the sensation produced by physical contact with
metal type.

Book jacket and binding
tan and black, Alfred Knopf
1945

The broadside text (Genesis creation/fall narrative, in numbered verses) reads:

1. Now the serpent was more subtle than any beast of the field which the Lord God had made. And he said unto the woman: 'Yea, hath God said: Ye shall not eat of any tree of the garden?'
2. And the woman said unto the serpent: 'Of the fruit of the trees of the garden we may eat;
3. but of the fruit of the tree which is in the midst of the garden, God hath said: Ye shall not eat of it, neither shall ye touch it, lest ye die.'
4. And the serpent said unto the woman: 'Ye shall not surely die;
5. for God doth know that in the day ye eat thereof, then your eyes shall be opened, and ye shall be as God, knowing good and evil.'

6. And when the woman saw that the tree was good for food, and that it was a delight to the eyes, and that the tree was to be desired to make one wise, she took of the fruit thereof, and did eat; and she gave also unto her husband with her, and he did eat.
7. And the eyes of them both were opened, and they knew that they were naked; and they sewed fig-leaves together, and made themselves girdles.
8. And they heard the voice of the Lord God walking in the garden toward the cool of the day; and the man and his wife hid themselves from the presence of the Lord God amongst the trees of the garden.

9. And the Lord God called unto the man, and said unto him: 'Where art thou?'
10. And he said: 'I heard Thy voice in the garden, and I was afraid, because I was naked; and I hid myself.'
11. And He said: 'Who told thee that thou wast naked? Hast thou eaten of the tree, whereof I commanded thee that thou shouldst not eat?'
12. And the man said: 'The woman whom Thou gavest to be with me, she gave me of the tree, and I did eat.'
13. And the Lord God said unto the woman: 'What is this thou hast done?' And the woman said: 'The serpent beguiled me, and I did eat.'

14. And the Lord God said unto the serpent: 'Because thou hast done this, cursed art thou from among all cattle, and from among all beasts of the field; upon thy belly shalt thou go, and dust shalt thou eat all the days of thy life.
15. And I will put enmity between thee and the woman, and between thy seed and her seed; they shall bruise thy head, and thou shalt bruise their heel.'
16. Unto the woman He said: 'I will greatly multiply thy pain and thy travail; in pain thou shalt bring forth children; and thy desire shall be to thy husband, and he shall rule over thee.'

17. And unto Adam He said: 'Because thou hast hearkened unto the voice of thy wife, and hast eaten of the tree, of which I commanded thee, saying: Thou shalt not eat of it; cursed is the ground for thy sake; in toil shalt thou eat of it all the days of thy life;
18. Thorns also and thistles shall it bring forth to thee; and thou shalt eat the herb of the field.
19. In the sweat of thy face shalt thou eat bread, till thou return unto the ground; for out of it wast thou taken; for dust thou art, and unto dust shalt thou return.'
20. And the man called his wife's name, Eve; because she was the mother of all living.

21. And the Lord God made for Adam and for his wife garments of skins, and clothed them.
22. And the Lord God said: 'Behold, the man is become as one of us, to know good and evil; and now, lest he put forth his hand, and take also of the tree of life, and eat, and live for ever.'
23. Therefore the Lord God sent him forth from the garden of Eden, to till the ground from whence he was taken.
24. So He drove out the man; and He placed at the east of the garden of Eden the cherubim, and the flaming sword which turned every way, to keep the way to the tree of life.

Design and typography: Paul Rand
Composition and offset printing: Tri-Arts Press
Text: 14 Linotype Garamond # 3
Paper: Clear Spring Brook, antique offset natural

…In ordering his space and in distributing his typographic material and symbols, he is able to predetermine, to a certain point, the eye movements of the spectator.

Broadside
full color, Westvaco
1968

Children's book
I Know a Lot of Things, Harcourt Brace
1956

A typeface which sometimes is described as having *character* often is merely bizarre, eccentric, nostalgic, or simply buckeye.

To distort the letters of the alphabet in 'the style of' Chinese calligraphy (sometimes referred to as chop suey lettering), because the subject happens to deal with the Orient is to create the typographic equivalent of a corny illustration. To mimic a woodcut style of type to 'go with' a woodcut; to use bold type to 'harmonize with' heavy machinery, etc. is cliche-thinking. The designer is unaware of the exciting possibilities inherent in the *contrast* of picture and type matter. Thus, instead of combining a woodcut with a 'woodcut style' of type (Neuland), a happier choice would be a more classical design (Caslon, Bodoni, or Helvetica) to achieve the element of surprise and to accentuate by contrast the form and character of both text and picture.

Logotype
Cresta Blanca Wine Co.
1942

In this logotype for Cresta Blanca wine (a product which ordinarily might suggest a more conventional type style, Didot or Spencerian, to evoke a sense of gentility and pedigree) simple, bold, sans-serif letters are combined with delicate line drawings. This contrast revitalizes—gives new meaning—to familiar images:

Newspaper advertisement
black and white, Ohrbach's
1946

By contrasting type and pictorial matter, the designer is able to create new combinations and elicit new meanings. For instance, in the Air-Wick newspaper advertisement, the old and the new are brought into harmony. This effect is achieved by contrasting two apparently unrelated subjects — 19th-century wood engravings and 20th-century typewriter type. The surrounding white space helps to separate the advertisement from its competitors, creates an illusion of greater size per square inch, and produces a sense of cleanliness and freshness.

... The isolated letter affords a means of visual expression which other kinds of imagery cannot quite duplicate. Letters in the forms of trademarks, seals, and monograms—on business forms, identification tags, athletic jerseys, or even handkerchiefs—possess some magical quality. They serve not only as status symbols but have the virtue of brevity as well.

Newspaper advertisement
Seeman Brothers
1944

with the sense of sight,
the idea communicates the emotion...
Alfred North Whitehead

Poster, full color
Advertising Typographers Association
1965

BC EF
GHIJK
LMNOPQ
RST V
WXY
Z

Building sign
aluminum
1957

Magazine cover
black and pink, AD Magazine
1941

abcdefghijklmnopqrstuvwxyz st
ABCDEFGHIJKLMNOPQRSTUVWXYZ
1234567890$¢ &!?.,:;-—""''( )

Alphabet design
Westinghouse
'1961

Bulb packages
blue and white, Westinghouse
1968

88

100

extra
life*
bulbs

 extra
life*
light
bulbs

7 FT 199 100
MADE IN USA

 extra
life*
light
bulbs

100 watt

Trademark
United Parcel Service
1961

90

A better means of nasal medication... In a recent survey, 77% of the pediatricians interviewed stated that they use Benzedrine Inhaler, N.N.R. in their practice. The Inhaler has achieved this widespread pediatric acceptance because: (1) children accept it willingly, and show none of the hostility which so often complicates the administration of drops, tampons and sprays; and (2) it does not give rise to any significant degree of secondary turgescence, atony, or bogginess when used as directed. Benzedrine Inhaler is strikingly effective in reducing the congestion of head colds, allergic rhinitis and sinusitis.

Benzedrine Inhaler, N. N. R.

Microform Sulfathiazole Suspension

A general-purpose fluid sulfonamide for local use... In pediatric practice, Microform Sulfathiazole Suspension, 20%, is pre-eminently useful in pyogenic skin infections and minor injuries. For example, Harris[?] employed this Suspension in the treatment of 15 children with impetigo contagiosa, and brought all lesions under control within a single day. Microform Sulfathiazole Suspension, 20%, offers: (1) enhanced therapeutic effect, due to the Microform (microcrystalline) sulfathiazole; (2) chemical stability and neutral pH; (3) deposition of a closely adherent, calamine-like blanket.

A revolutionary advance in intranasal sulfonamide therapy...because it provides vasoconstriction in minutes and bacteriostasis for hours, Paredrine-Sulfathiazole Suspension is prescribed by many pediatricians. Of this outstanding vasoconstrictor-sulfonamide, Livingston[?] in the "Proceedings" of the twelfth annual meeting of the American Academy of Pediatrics, states:
"This suspension...may shorten the course of the common cold and tend to prevent complications." Investigators have noted the "absence of clumping and of irritation, and negligible absorption into the blood stream. They...obtained excellent results."

Paredrine-Sulfathiazole Suspension

...The numeral as a means of expression possesses many of the same qualities as the letter. It can also be the visual equivalent of time, space, position, and quantity; and it can help to impart to a printed piece a sense of rhythm and immediacy.

Folder
full color, SKF Laboratories
1945

desi8n 63

Poster, tan on white
N.Y. Art Directors Club
1963

...Punctuation marks, as emotive, plastic symbols, have served the artist as a means of expression in painting as well as in the applied arts.

Booklet
red, black, and green, U.S. Government
1943

Coco, mostraram, aos fazendeiros, o primeiro arado que, jamais, viram. No futuro, as refeições, destes fazendeiros, serão melhores.

Os Homens:

Estes variados planos que dizem respeito à saúde, reconstrução e alimentação, são orientados por homens competentes, cujas funções variam, desde as negociações com o governo, até a edificação de hospitais de seis andares, desde da montagem de mosquiteiros à organização da Indústria da fibra; desde o trabalho de exterminar ratos, por meio de lança-chamas, à construção de acampamentos para trabalhadores.

Os homens, que realizam este mister, devem saber como enfrentar terremotos, incêndios, enchentes, secas, cobras, pulgas, arraias venenosas, peixes elétricos, vampiros, formigas carnívoras . . . e a propaganda nazista.

Entre estes profissionais, se encontram diplomatas, contadores, sanitaristas, economistas, engenheiros sanitaristas, especialistas em medicina tropical, enfermeiras e fazendeiros, cujo objetivo é proporcionar um padrão de vida mais elevado, para todas as Américas.

Em uma palavra, o objetivo, destes pioneiros e colaboradores, é estabelecer ambiente social em que o simples cidadão, irritado com meras palavras, possa conseguir uma refeição substancial, quando faminto, e cuidado médico, quando doente; sim, um ambiente social em que todos vivamos uma vida digna de ser vivida. **O Homem, Quanto Vale?**

...Para nós, nas vinte e uma repúblicas da América, ele vale tudo

Booklet
red, black, and green, U. S. Government
1943

Where the basic appeals of visual communication can be interpreted most graphically by abandoning the literal approach, it is the artist's business to do so. If he translates them into a visual message which is not only arresting and persuasive, but imaginative, dramatic, and entertaining as well, he has fulfilled his obligation to his audience; and perhaps he has also fulfilled his obligation to more personal standards.

Even if it is true that the average man seems most comfortable with the commonplace and familiar, it is equally true that catering to bad taste, which we so readily attribute to the average reader, merely perpetuates that mediocrity and denies the reader one of the most easily accessible means for esthetic development and eventual enjoyment.

Book jacket
black and pink, Alfred Knopf
1945

Titles in this Series
Edited by John Lewis FSIA